Counting with Friends OUTSIDE

By

Miss Sasha

This book is dedicated to the
Sharpe kids, my love for books
and my love for children...
especially my Darian.

A special acknowledgement
and huge thank you to
Cassie Johnson
for her artistic contribution.

Contact info: Instagram Follow_This_Brush

1 sun shining brightly in the sky

2 birds

flying together side by side

3 bees buzzing as loudly as can be

4 apples growing upon an apple tree

5 ducks
swimming
in a pond
so blue

6 beautiful butterflies and their colorful wings too

7 gray rocks sitting perfectly still

8 tiny ants climbing up a hill

9 flowers blooming underneath the sun

10 children playing and having so much fun

The End